LINES ON THE UNDERGROUND

*an anthology
for Metropolitan and Hammersmith &
City Line travellers*

Compiled by

DOROTHY MEADE & TATIANA WOLFF

Illustrated by Jonathan Newdick

CASSELL

To Joe, Dora, Anna and Ben

*

And in memory of
M. M. W.

Cassell Publishers Limited
Wellington House, 125 Strand
London WC2R 0BB

in association with the London Transport Museum

Selection
copyright © Dorothy Meade and Tatiana Wolff 1994, 1996
Extracts copyright authors and publishers (see Acknowledgements)
Illustrations copyright © Jonathan Newdick 1994

This edition published 1996
The material in this anthology was first published in
Lines on the Underground, 1994

British Library Cataloguing in Publication Data
A catalogue record for this book is available from the British Library

ISBN 0-304-34862-7

Distributed in Australia by
Capricorn Link (Australia) Pty Ltd
2/13 Carrington Road, Castle Hill, NSW 2154

Printed and bound in Great Britain by Hillman Printers Ltd

METROPOLITAN LINE

Aldgate

The western approaches to the walled City of London were . . . magnif-
icent, but to the east it was a very different story, for as the houses of
the traders and shopkeepers grew larger and more dignified, the poor
retreated to their own suburbs. Eastward, beyond the bars of Aldgate,
Stow writes that '. . . in some places it scarce remaineth sufficient high-
way for the meeting of carriages and droves of cattle: much less is there
any fair, pleasant, or wholesome way for people to walk on foot,
which is no small blemish to so famous a city to have so unsavoury
and unseemly an entrance or passage thereunto'.

MARY CATHCART BORER, *The City of London: A History*, 1977

Liverpool Street

Change for Central, Circle and Hammersmith & City lines

This is the most picturesque and interesting of the London Termini. It
has the most varied users. Blond, blue-eyed and large . . . the Scandin-
avians and Dutch arrive from Harwich on the boat train. A few
Belgians and French who come by air to Southend Airport get in at the
nearest Essex station. . . . The county families, farmers, vicars, and agri-
cultural manufacturers come in from Norfolk, East Suffolk and outer
Essex, from the Gainsborough, Crome and Constable landscapes of
flint church towers, deep red brick manor houses, willows, elms, malt
houses and mills. . . . You find yourself on an elevated walk, a long and
attractive one. . . . This high walk all under the roof of the station takes
you past the original English yellow brick-and-stone Gothic of the
Great Eastern's first effort into the really spendid vista of columns and
iron roofs of what most people mean by Liverpool Street Station. The
Great Eastern wanted their train shed to be Cathedral-like as the buildings. . . . Double columns support the two main aisles. Beyond these
are yet further aisles. The eastward view is enlivened by a delightful
verandah fret, outlined black against the grey east-London sky. . . . By
some great good fortune a sister teashop to what is now the
Stationmaster's office remains perched on our upland walk. I know no

greater pleasure for elevenses in London than to sit in this tea place and watch the trains arrive and depart.

JOHN BETJEMAN, *London's Historic Railway Stations*, 1972

Moorgate

Change for Circle and Northern lines

When I was small I ran away
    And through the Moor-gate tried to stray
    To pick a bunch of heather;
But there a man paced to and fro
In garments that were white as snow,
    Though he was brown as leather.

His sword was like the sickle moon,
He stood up in his scarlet shoon
    Taller than any other!
He laid his finger on his breast,
And he looked East, so I ran West
    Crying for my Mother.

ELEANOR FARJEON, *Nursery Rhymes of London Town*, 1917

Barbican

When the great bell
BOOMS over the Portland stone urn, and
From the carved cedar wood
Rises the odour of incense,
I SIT DOWN
In St. Botolph Bishopsgate Churchyard
And wait for the spirit of my grandfather
Toddling along from the Barbican.

JOHN BETJEMAN, 'City', *Continual Dew*, 1937

Farringdon

I sallied out, down Holborn, and turned down Farringdon Street. . . . There are in this street one or two places used as headquarters for the stage waggons – the old six-horsed Saxon wains, with low broad wheels and hoop canopies. When laden and in motion they look like haystacks covered with tarpaulin, and rumbling on wheels. They have a tremendous difficulty to surmount on starting – to get up Holborn Hill. I have often watched them here – seen all the muscles of eight stout horses on the stretch for seven or eight minutes, to move one of these wains a distance of about thirty yards.

JOHN TOWNE DANSON, *Economic and Statistical
Studies 1840-1890*, 1906

At FARRINGDON that lunch hour at a stall
He bought a dozen plants of London Pride;
While she, in arc-lit Oxford Street adrift,
Soared through the sales by safe hydraulic lift.

JOHN BETJEMAN, 'The Metropolitan Railway – Baker Street Station Buffet',
A Few Late Chrysanthemums, 1954

King's Cross St. Pancras
Change for Circle, Hammersmith & City, Northern, Piccadilly and Victoria lines

Boadicea rallied her forces and sacked Colchester, London and St Albans, leaving in her wake seventy thousand Roman dead. . . . When the two armies met, the Iceni were overwhelmingly defeated, their dead outnumbering those of the Romans by two hundred to one. Boadicea and her daughters promptly swallowed poison. She lies buried somewhere under Platform 10 at King's Cross Station.

PETER BUSHELL, *London's Secret History*, 1983

Even when he had bought his ticket, a first-class that he could hardly afford, in the leisurely fashion demanded by such an act of self-indulgence, and had loitered at the kiosks buying papers and a tin of tobacco, Adam Stewart discovered that he had still some twenty minutes or so left. Not that it mattered; they would soon pass. He found himself repeating, with the solemn relish of one who achieves nonsense, 'Pancrastination is the thief of time.' St. Pancras, surely the most canonical of all our stations, seemed to rebuke his levity. Indignant puffs of smoke and steam, sudden red glares of anger, ascended to the great arched roof. The locomotives grunted and wheezed like outraged sacristans. The thin high voices of the newsboys ran together into a protesting chorus of virgins and elders. But no, that was Greek drama, Adam reminded himself, and nothing to do with cathedrals, and it is with cathedrals that large railway stations must always be compared.

J.B. PRIESTLEY, *Adam in Moonshine*, 1927

Dr Haldane sought out a pharmacist in Gower Street who had for many years dispensed his own 'Metropolitan Mixture' to ease the plight of persons emerging in distress from the nearby station.*

*A visit to this shop is described in a letter to *The Times*, 14 June 1879. The victim reported himself as instantly diagnosed: – 'Oh! I see – Metropolitan Railway!' As he gratefully downed the medicine, he was told by the pharmacist that he often treated up to twenty cases a day.

ALAN A. JACKSON, *London's Metropolitan Railway*, 1986

Euston Square

It was a railway passenger,
  And he leapt out jauntilie.
'Now up and bear, thou stout portèr,
  My two chattèls to me.

Bring hither, bring hither my bag so red,
  And portmanteau so brown:
(They lie in the van, for a trusty man
  He labelled them London town.)

And fetch me eke a cabman bold,
  That I may be his fare, his fare;
And he shall have a good shilling,
  If by two of the clock he do me bring
  To the Terminus, Euston Square.'

C.S. CALVERLEY, 'Striking', *Verses and Translations*, 1862

'The first Pullman cars in Europe to be hauled by electricity.'

'No, really? The first in Europe?' I was almost as interested as I pretended to be.

'The first in Europe. There's a lot of history in this line, you know. Heard of John Stuart Mill?'

'Yes.' (Of course not).

'Do you know what his last speech in the House was about?'

I think I must have shown that I didn't.

'The House of Commons. His last speech? It was about the Underground. Can you imagine that? The Railway Regulation Bill, 1868. An amendment was moved to the bill making it obligatory for all railways to attach a smoking carriage to their trains. Mill got the bill through. Made a great speech in favour of it. Carried the day.'

'Jolly good. It was jolly good wasn't it?'

'But – guess what – there was one railway, just one, that was exempted. That *was the Metropolitan.'*

'Why ?'

'Ah. Because of the smoke in the tunnels. It's always been a bit special, you see.'

JULIAN BARNES, *Metroland*, 1980

Great Portland Street

I remember well, when I was in my eighth year [1774], Mr Nollekens calling at my father's house in Great Portland Street, to see the notorious Jack Rann, commonly called Sixteen-String Jack, go to Tyburn to be hanged. . . . The criminal was dressed in a pea-green coat with an immense nosegay in his button-hole, which had been presented to him at St Sepulchre's steps; and his nankeen small-clothes, we were told, were tied at each knee with sixteen strings. [Jack had boasted that his sixteen strings represented the sixteen times he had been tried and acquitted.]

J.T. SMITH, *A Book for a Rainy Day*, 1905 edition

November 6th 1863. To Hatton Garden by the Metropolitan Railway to get me a stronger pair of spectacles. Never saw the underground rail before; it gives one the idea of going into an immense, tidy coal cellar, did not strike cold but smelt rather sepulchral.

LOUISA BAIN quoted in *A Bookseller Looks Back*, J.S. Bain, 1940

Baker Street
Change for Bakerloo, Circle, Jubilee and Hammersmith & City lines

This plaque marks the restoration of Baker Street Station platforms 5 & 6. The two platforms were part of the world's first underground railway which opened in 1863 between Paddington and Farringdon. Unveiled by R.M. Robbins, April 1984

Plaque at Baker Street Station

As we came up at Baker Street,
Where tubes and trains and 'buses meet
There's a touch of fog and a touch of sleet;
And we go on up Hampstead way
Towards the closing of the day. . . .

But here we are in the Finchley Road
With a drizzling rain and a skidding 'bus
And the twilight settling down on us.

FORD MADOX HUEFFER, 'Finchley Road',
Songs from London, 1916

Finchley Road
Change for Jubilee line

I had now arrived at that particular point of my walk where four roads met – the road to Hampstead, along which I had returned, the road to Finchley, the road to West End, and the road back to London. I had mechanically turned in this latter direction, and was strolling along the lonely highroad – idly wondering, I remember, what the Cumberland young ladies would look like – when, in one moment, every drop of blood in my body was brought to a stop by the touch of a hand laid lightly and suddenly on my shoulder from behind me.

I turned on the instant, with my fingers tightening round the handle of my stick.

There, in the middle of the broad, bright highroad – there, as if it had that moment sprung out of the earth or dropped from the heaven – stood the figure of a solitary Woman, dressed from head to foot in white garments, her face bent in grave inquiry on mine, her hand pointing to the dark cloud over London, as I faced her.

8

I was far too seriously startled by the suddenness with which this extraordinary apparition stood before me, in the dead of night and in that lonely place, to ask what she wanted. The strange woman spoke first.

'Is that the road to London?' she said . . .

'Yes,' I replied, 'that is the way: it leads to St John's Wood and the Regent's Park.'

WILKIE COLLINS, *The Woman in White*, 1860

Now in the evening, after work,
We race into the gathering murk
Together, on the Child's Hill bus,
While all the stars smile down on us –
I and my love, and London nights,
Sufficient for our naive delights!

DOUGLAS GOLDRING, 'Finchley Road', *Streets*, 1912

Wembley Park
Change for Jubilee line

Wembley Park . . . originated as a private estate owned by Richard Page for whom it was landscaped by Humphrey Repton in 1793. The Metropolitan Railway passed through the park in 1880 and the whole estate was acquired by the Railway Company in 1889 for a leisure centre for north-west London.

The London Encyclopaedia edited by Ben Weinreb
and Christopher Hibbert, 1983

Preston Road

Smoothly from HARROW, passing PRESTON ROAD,
  They saw the last green fields and misty sky,
At NEASDEN watched a workmen's train unload,
  And, with the morning villas sliding by,
They felt so sure on their electric trip
That Youth and Progress were in partnership.

JOHN BETJEMAN, 'The Metropolitan Railway – Baker Street Station Buffet',
A Few Late Chrysanthemums, 1954

Northwick Park

From then on, I was not only interested in my journey, but proud of it. The termitary of Kilburn; the grimy, lost stations between Baker Street and Finchley Road; the steppe-like playing-fields at Northwick Park; the depot at Neasden, full of idle, aged rolling-stock; the frozen faces of passengers glimpsed in the windows of fast Marylebone trains. They were all, in some way, relevant, fulfilling, sensibility-sharpening. And what was life about if not that?

JULIAN BARNES, *Metroland*, 1980

Harrow-on-the-Hill
Change for Amersham, Chesham and Watford branches

I wish to be buried in Harrow church: there is a spot in the church-yard, near the footpath, on the brow of the hill looking towards Windsor, and a tomb under a large tree (bearing the name of Peachie, or Peachey), where I used to sit for hours and hours when a boy: this was my favourite spot.

LORD BYRON, letter to John Murray, 26 May 1822,
from Montenero near Leghorn

Ye scenes of my childhood, whose loved recollection
　　Embitters the present, compared with the past;
Where science first dawn'd on the powers of reflection,
　　And friendships were form'd, too romantic to last. . . .
Again, I behold where for hours I have ponder'd,
　　As reclining, at eve, on yon tombstone I lay;
Or round the steep brow of the churchyard I wander'd
　　To catch the last gleam of the sun's setting ray.

LORD BYRON, 'On a distant view of the village and school of
Harrow on the Hill', *Hours of Idleness*, 1807

Harrow-on-the-Hill is in the middle of the suburbs: the tomb in the Parish churchyard where Byron once lay and composed poetry as he looked over rolling meadows now commands a fine view of the semis of Hillingdon and Pinner. It was only a few stops from Baker Street on the Metropolitan Line and we used to sit in the smoke-filled carriages to be jeered at as we went up to Lord's, dressed in top hat, pearl-grey waistcoat, morning coat and silver-topped stick with a dark-blue tassel. We weren't allowed to speak to the boys at the bottom of the hill, although a Prefect might occasionally give one of them sixpence to carry up his suitcase at the beginning of term.

JOHN MORTIMER, *Clinging to the Wreckage*, 1982

UXBRIDGE BRANCH

West Harrow
Turn to page 15 for North Harrow

The parish church of Harrow, from its situation on the summit of a hill . . . is an object unusually conspicuous, and cannot fail to attract the notice of all who travel along the North Western Railway. It is recorded that when some divines were disputing with King Charles II about the *visible Church*, his Majesty said that he 'knew not where it was to be found, except, indeed, at Harrow'.

E. WALFORD, *Greater London*, 1882–4

'I love Harrow,' said Sir John Betjeman recently, 'first because it is not Eton and secondly because I believe I was at school there . . . in spirit if not in fact.'

I find no surprise that he should say so . . . and also for two reasons: first because it is one of the most complete, compact and unspoiled complexes of Victorian architecture in the country, and second because it is visibly, if not in fact, the capital city of Metroland – that strange Arcady that was the product, some fifty years ago, of a partnership between the Metropolitan Railway and the speculative builder.

HUGH CASSON, *Hugh Casson's London*, 1983

I have very early recollections of the various Underground railways – all electrified by 1902 – and of their biscuit-coloured basket-work seats, their swaying straps, the constant smell of hot metal from (I supposed) the 'live rail', and the shouts of the guards – one guard to every other carriage.

C.H. ROLPH, *London Particulars*, 1980

Rayners Lane
Change for Piccadilly line

It was at the lonely spot of Rayners Lane [1923] where the Metropolitan had a junction with the District Railway (so bleak in winter, that the windswept platforms were known as Pneumonia Junction) that the first large-scale housing development took place. . . . Another advertisement for three Nash houses claimed that 'living in Rayners Lane would be all peace and quiet, a place where the din and turmoil of the streets are exchanged for an aspect of spreading landscapes . . . of trees and green pastures where the only sounds are of birds . . .'. Growth was rapid: in 1930, Rayners Lane station was handling 22,000 passengers a year. By 1937 the total was a staggering four million!

DENNIS EDWARDS AND RON PIGRAM,
London's Underground Suburbs, 1986

Eastcote

The days of the great School Treat were still with us in the 1900s – a Victorian children's outing for a year of good attendance at Sunday School or day school – and went on well into the Thirties.

In west London children were taken on highly organised outings . . . to the countryside at Ruislip or Eastcote.

DENNIS EDWARDS AND RON PIGRAM,
London's Underground Suburbs, 1986

'Où habites-tu?' *they would ask year after year, drilling us for French orals; and always I would smirkingly reply,*
. 'J'habite Metroland.'
It sounded better than Eastwick, stranger than Middlesex; more like a concept in the mind than a place where you shopped. And so, of course, it was. As the Metropolitan Railway had pushed westward in the 1880s, a thin corridor of land was opened up with no geographical or ideological unity; you lived there because it was an area easy to get out of. The name Metroland – adopted during the First World War both by estate agents and the railway itself – gave the string of rural suburbs a spurious integrity.

JULIAN BARNES, *Metroland*, 1980

Ruislip Manor

And all that day in murky London Wall
The thought of RUISLIP kept him warm inside . . .

JOHN BETJEMAN, 'The Metropolitan Railway – Baker Street
Station Buffet', *A Few Late Chrysanthemums*, 1984

Ruislip

Even those who feel a preference for the delights of man-made civilisa-
tion invariably find that if their days are to be spent in the big city,
they are happy to return, in the quiet dusk of the evenings, to nature's
stronghold outside the town, enthused the Manor Homes brochure. At
Ruislip each house was 'a palace in miniature' and prices started at
£450 for a two-bedroomed home – with weekly repayments of 12s.6d.
[62^1/$_2$p] after a £5 deposit.

DENNIS EDWARDS AND RON PIGRAM,
London's Underground Suburbs, 1986

*The tricks of travel were learned early. How to fold a full-sized newspaper verti-
cally so that you could turn over in the width of one page. How to pretend you
hadn't seen the sort of women you were expected to stand up for. Where to
stand in a full train to get the best chance of a seat when it began to empty.
Where to get on a train so that you got off at just the right spot. How to use the
no-exit tunnels for short cuts.*

JULIAN BARNES, *Metroland*, 1980

Ickenham

So we together merrily to Swakely [Ickenham], Sir R. Viner's – a very
pleasant place . . . He showed me a black boy that he had that died of a
consumption; and being dead, he caused him to be dried in a Oven,
and lies there entire in a box. By and by to dinner.

SAMUEL PEPYS, *Diary, 7 September 1665*

Hillingdon

The Red Lion entertained Charles I as an unwilling guest after his escape from Oxford, with Dr Michael Hudson, his chaplain, and Mr Ashburnham, one of his grooms of the bedchamber, in April 1646:

After we had passed Uxbridge at one Mr. Teasdale's house a taverne in Hillingdon, we alighted & stayed to refresh ourselves, betwixt 10 and 11 of the Clocke; & there stayed two or three hours: where the King was much perplexed what Course to resolve upon, London, or North-ward? The Considerations of the former Vote, & the apparent Danger of being discovered at London, moved him to resolve at last to go North-ward, & through Norfolke, where he was least knowne. . . . About 2 of the clocke we tooke a Guide towards Barnet, resolving to crosse the Roads into Essex. But, after we were passed Harrow upon the Hill, I told the King, if we were not knowne much in S. Albon's road, it was much the nearer Way to go thro' S. Albons, & thence towards Royston, which he approved of. And so we passed through S. Albons, where one old Man with an Halberd asked us, whence we came? I told him, from the Parliament; and threw him 6d & soe passed.

FRANCIS PECK, *Desiderata Curiosa*, vol. ii, lib. IX, 21, 1735

Uxbridge

It is supposed by some that, like Oxford, the town derived its name from the number of oxen continually passing through it from Buckinghamshire and the western counties on their way up to London.

E. WALFORD, *Greater London*, 1882–4

On Thursday 30th June 1904 the Metropolitan laid on a lavish opening ceremony for its new line to Uxbridge. A special train, hauled by 0-0-4T no 1, gaily decorated with flags and evergreens, its coal painted white, was worked from Baker Street to South Harrow and Uxbridge. Luncheon was then served in a marquee in Uxbridge Station yard, where two of the new Metropolitan electric stock trailer cars were parked for inspection by the guests. It was evidently a very pleasant day, for a journey that would be unrecognisable to present residents of the area . . . bathed in glorious sunshine and scented with new mown hay, the countryside was at its best. Here stretches of meadowland, with herds of sleek cattle grazing lazily, there the clink and rattle of grass-cutting machines. Plump partridges raised their startled heads and a pheasant, with the glorious plumage shining like burnished gold, ran for cover.

Middlesex & Buckinghamshire Advertiser, 2 July 1904, quoted in *London's Metropolitan Railway* by Alan A. Jackson, 1986

AMERSHAM AND CHESHAM BRANCHES

North Harrow

By 1914, the western end of Harrow had reached out along the Pinner road mainly by the efforts of local builder Albert Cutler. . . .

Living at North Harrow was given an extra air of security by one of Cutler's advertisements: 'Many of our houses have been purchased by surveyors, bankers and architects.' No doubt they were attracted by the superb stained-glass windows in every hall and landing. There was a choice of designs: sailing ships; lighthouses and seagulls; windmills; and the inevitable sunrise. Surely, these rows of semi-detached houses in their narrow road overhung by flowering trees, the gardens full of rustic trellis and roses, capture the very essence of Metro-land.

DENNIS EDWARDS AND RON PIGRAM,
London's Underground Suburbs, 1986

Pinner

There was an Old Person of Pinner,
As thin as a lath, if not thinner;
    They dressed him in white,
    And roll'd him up tight,
That elastic Old Person of Pinner.

EDWARD LEAR, *More Nonsense, Pictures,
Rhymes, Botany, etc.*,1872

Early Electric! Sit you down and see,
　'Mid this fine woodwork and a smell of dinner,
A stained glass windmill and a pot of tea,
　And sepia views of leafy lanes in PINNER,
Then visualise far down the shining lines,
Your parents' homestead set in murmuring pines.

JOHN BETJEMAN, 'Metropolitan Railway – Baker Street Station Buffet',
A Few Late Chrysanthemums, 1954

Pinner, a parish of a thousand souls,
'Til the railways gave it many thousand more.
Pinner is famous for its village Fair
Where once a year, St John the Baptist's Day,
Shows all the climbing High Street filled with stalls.
It is the Feast Day of the Parish Saint,
A medieval Fair in Metro-land.

JOHN BETJEMAN, 'Metro-Land' (TV programme), 1973, quoted in
The Best of Betjeman selected by John Guest, 1978

Northwood Hills

Oh, for the rolling Northwood Hills, the wild places of Ongar and the
savage ravines of Gants Hill. The names are as evocative and remote as
Persepolis and Samarkand.

PHILIP HOWARD, *The Times*

Northwood

. . . the most ambitious Metropolitan suburb along the 'Extension' Line
was between Pinner and Northwood. Here there were open fields until
1930, when two business men, H. Peachey and Harry Neal, produced
plans for a completely new suburb. A competition was held to find a
name through the local press. The winner of the £5 prize was a lady
from North Harrow with 'Northwood Hills'. . . .

Houses soon began creeping up muddy Porridge Pot Hill, which was
renamed Potter Street for suburban tastes . . . the first residents in the
chill of winter were not completely happy. . . . 'I arrived at a station,'
wrote one early Metro-land pioneer, 'and stepped into mud of the

most adhesive quality I had ever seen or felt yet I was to find that residing in a suburb adds a thrill and a zest to life. It is an experience in having no tradition to live up to.'

DENNIS EDWARDS AND RON PIGRAM,
London's Underground Suburbs, 1986

It is a comfort to those that never go farther out than the central warren of the London Underground that the roots of their system stretch out to the country where rabbits roam and stockbrokers play golf.

PHILIP HOWARD, *The Times*

Moor Park

Did ever Golf Club have a nineteenth hole
So sumptuous as this?
Did ever Golf Club have so fine a hall?
Venetian decor, 1732.

And yonder dome is not a dome at all
But painted in the semblance of a dome;
The sculptured figures all are done in paint
That lean towards us with so rapt a look.
How skilfully the artist takes us in.

What Georgian wit these classic Gods have heard,
Who now must listen to the golfer's tale
Of holes in one and how I missed that putt,
Hooked at the seventh, sliced across the tenth
But ended on the seventeenth all square.

Ye gods, ye gods, how comical we are!
Would Jove have been appointed Captain here?
See how exclusive thine Estate, Moor Park.

JOHN BETJEMAN, 'Metro-Land' (TV programme), 1973, quoted in
The Best of Betjeman selected by John Guest, 1978

Rickmansworth

Rickmansworth was in the early Middle Ages Ryke-meres-wearth; that is, a rich moor-meadow; and indeed the characteristic features of the town are its rivers, lakes, and water-meadows.

NIKOLAUS PEVSNER, *The Buildings of England: Hertfordshire*, 1953

Chorleywood

Above the seats were sepia photographs of the line's beauty spots – Sandy Lodge Golf Course, Pinner Hill, Moor Park, Chorley Wood. Most of the original fittings remained: wide, loosely strung luggage racks with coat-hooks curving down from their support struts; broad leather window straps, and broad leather straps to stop the doors from swinging all the way back on their hinges; a chunky, gilded figure on the door, 1 or 3; a brass fingerplate backing the brass door handle; and, engraved on the plate, in a tone of either command or seductive invitation, the slogan 'Live in Metroland'.

Over the years I studied the rolling stock. From the platform I could tell at a glance a wide from an extra-wide compartment. I knew all the advertisements by heart, and all the varieties of decoration on the barrel-vaulted ceilings. I knew the range of imagination of the people who scraped the NO SMOKING transfers on the windows into new mottos: NO SNORING was the most popular piece of knife-work; NO SNOGGING a baffler for years; NO SNOWING the most whimsical. I stowed away in a first-class carriage one dark afternoon, and sat bolt upright in the soft seat, too frightened to look around me. I even penetrated, by mistake, the special single compartment at the front of each train, which was protected by a green transfer LADIES ONLY. Having only just caught my connection, I fell panting into the silent disapproval of three tweeded ladies; though my fear was cooled less by their silence than by my disappointment that the compartment contained no special appurtenances indicative, however obliquely, of just what it was that made women different.

JULIAN BARNES, *Metroland*, 1980

Chalfont & Latimer

John Milton came here [Chalfont St Giles] in 1665 to escape the Great Plague of London and complete *Paradise Lost*. . . .

Chalfont St Giles, in the Burnham Hundred, is part of the famous Chiltern Hundreds. Sir Robert Peel and Roy Jenkins are among the many Members of Parliament who have sought the now traditional appointment of 'Steward or Bailiff of Her Majesty's three Chiltern Hundreds of Stoke, Desborough and Burnham' so as to be able to relinquish membership of the House of Commons.

LEIGH HATTS, *Country Walks around London*, 1983

Amersham

Steam took us onwards, through the ripening fields,
Ripe for development. Where the landscape yields
Clay for warm brick, timber for post and rail,
Through Amersham to Aylesbury and the Vale.
In those wet fields the railway didn't pay,
The Metro stops at Amersham today.

JOHN BETJEMAN, 'Metro-Land' (TV programme), 1973, quoted in
The Best of Betjeman selected by John Guest, 1978

* * *

Chesham

In the early 1960s, the Metropolitan Line (by which the purist naturally meant the Watford, Chesham and Amersham branches) still retained some of its original separateness. The rolling-stock, painted a distinctive mid-brown, had remained unchanged for sixty years; some of the bogeys my Ian Allen spotter's book informed me, had been running since the early 1890s. The carriages were high and square, with broad wooden running-boards; the compartments were luxuriously wide by modern standards, and the breadth of the seats made one marvel at Edwardian femural development. The backs of the seats were raked at an angle which implied that in the old days the trains had stopped for longer at the stations.

JULIAN BARNES, *Metroland*, 1980

Croxley

In 1931 METROLAND described the area: 'Croxley bids fair to grow rapidly. Till lately it was somewhat difficult of access; its inhabitants are now offered almost a superabundance of transport facilities.' But the suburb was not built up very much before 1939 and even now is bordered by some attractive country.

> DENNIS EDWARDS AND RON PIGRAM,
> *London's Underground Suburbs*, 1986

Watford

Watford has . . . spread and sprawled. It is no longer a market town. The old High Street where at No. 288 my grandmother kept shop, is now the margin of the town. I went back to Watford a few years ago . . . the house where we spent our holidays, had been newly demolished. The two other houses in that little part of the street were still standing. For some reason on the site of the demolished building someone had planted a row of roses. They were young plants and looked as though they were freshly placed. It was mysterious to me to see those roses flourishing on the place where my grandparents flourished, kept shop, brought up their children and welcomed their granchildren. The flowers seemed to have been planted in their honour, but that was a fantasy – my grandparents were dead so long ago, and other tenants had taken their place. On that day I could almost hear my grandfather's voice again, as he mounted the creaky stairs with a cup of morning tea in his hand. 'Wake up . . .'

My grandparents' parlance often retained some flavour of the eighteenth century. Adelaide Uezzell didn't go for a walk, she 'went abroad'. As she kept a shop and had little time for household chores she sent the bed and table linen out to be washed. My grandfather, Tom, referred to this as 'the larndry'. I have heard elderly English people pronounce it so well into the 1940s.

> MURIEL SPARK, *Curriculum Vitae*, 1992

HAMMERSMITH & CITY LINE

A dark purplish-red, or burgundy, is the colour of the Metropolitan, green of the District, yellow of the Circle, scarlet of the Central, brown of the Bakerloo, dark blue of the Piccadilly and black of the Northern. These are the colours of lines on Beck's map and also sometimes of station trims and new station bucket seats.

On the map the Victoria Line became light blue. When the Jubilee Line was nearly finished there was some speculation as to what colour would be used for it. Possibilities remaining were pink, lime green, orange and mauve.

London Transport Underground chose grey.

Pink has been given, unexpectedly and without precedent, to the Hammersmith branch of the Metropolitan [now the Hammersmith & City Line].

BARBARA VINE, *King Solomon's Carpet*, 1991

Hammersmith
Change for District and Piccadilly lines

Saturday night! Saturday night!
I want to make Hammersmith hum.

A.P. HERBERT, 'Saturday Night', *Plain Jane*, 1927

The river flows before my door,
Sad with sea-gulls, mute with mud
Past Hammersmith and Castelnau,
And strung with barges at the flood.
Pink rowing girls by eight and four
Gently stroke the tide of blood.

A railway runs from side to side
And trains clank over on the hour.

GAVIN EWART, 'Tennysonian Reflections at Barnes Bridge',
Londoners, 1964

Goldhawk Road

Goldhawk Road was the original site of the Queen Charlotte's Maternity Hospital, which was founded in 1739 and was the earliest lying-in hospital in the British Isles.

Shepherd's Bush
Change for Central line

The philanthropic interest which brought Dickens so often to Hammersmith was a home for the rehabilitation of prostitutes, founded and maintained by Angela Burdett Coutts (1814–1906) at Shepherd's Bush. Dickens, who was a life-long friend and adviser of the wealthy and philanthropic Miss Coutts, not only planned the organisation of the Home, but also chose the house where it was to be lodged . . . on the Acton Road. . . . The name of the house was Urania Cottage. . . .

For many years after its establishment in 1847 Dickens took the closest interest in the Home, advising Miss Coutts on every aspect of the venture, from the choosing of the girls, staff and educational syllabus, down to the minutest detail of the daily running of the Home: all of which is reflected in his many letters to Miss Coutts. . . .

The customary drab workhouse clothes were not acceptable to Dickens. . . . 'Colour' he said 'is what these people always want, and colour (as allied to fancy), I would always give them. . . . Derry [a kind of cotton cloth] might just as well break out into stripe, or put forth a bud, or even burst into a full blown flower. Who is Derry that he is to make quakers of us all, whether we will or no!'

MOLLY TATCHELL, *Leigh Hunt and His Family in Hammersmith*, 1969

Latimer Road

The road is named after Edward Latymer [1557–1626/7] who bequeathed most of his lands to the parishes [in Hammersmith and Edmonton] to the end that the deserving boys should be put to school 'to keep them from vagrant courses' and where, as Latymer specified in his will, the boys should be taught to read English and receive instruction in some part of God's true religion.'*

* The Latymer School was originally housed in Fulham and moved to Hammersmith in 1648. This was to become the Latymer Upper School.

W. WHEATLEY, *The History of Edward Latymer and His Foundations*, 1936, revised 1953

The district to the north [of the town of Kensington] was very rural, and until the beginning of the nineteenth century had undergone little change for ages. Although it was scarcely three miles from London, the traveller could imagine himself in the most remote part of the country. The main road passing through this locality is now represented by Latimer Road. At the end of Pottery Lane was a colony of pig-keepers, and every house had a collection of pigs in its yard. A number of carts filled with tubs passed daily to London gathering refuse from hotels and mansions to provide food for the large families of pigs gathered here.

HAROLD CLUNN, *The Face of London*, 1932

Ladbroke Grove

Notting Hill, you may not know it, derives its distinctive street plan from the racecourse which finally bankrupted its developer . . . he had come to live in Notting Hill totally in ignorance of the fact that a ghostly imprint of a racecourse lay over its streets.

He did not hear the thunder of two-year-olds down Lansdowne Road. He did not see mud fly in the right turn on Stanley Crescent. He saw the name of Ladbroke, of course. You cannot miss a Ladbroke in Notting Hill. It is there on Square and Road and Terrace. But Ladbroke's was not yet a famous firm of London bookmakers and if the street names were coded messages from the future, Oscar did not know how to read them.

PETER CAREY, *Oscar and Lucinda*, 1988

Westbourne Park

One vivid contrast hung in his mind symbolical. On the one hand were the coalies of the Westbourne Park yards, on strike and gaunt and hungry, children begging in the black slush, and starving loungers outside a soup kitchen; and on the other, Westbourne Grove, two streets further, a blazing array of crowded shops, a stirring traffic of cabs and carriages, and such a spate of spending that a tired student in leaky boots and graceless clothes hurrying home was continually impeded in the whirl of skirts and parcels and sweetly pretty womanliness.

H.G. WELLS, *Love and Mr Lewisham*, 1900

Royal Oak

. . . the name of an old rural tavern, the entrance to which was by way of a wooden plank over the Westbourne River.

CYRIL M. HARRIS, *What's in a Name?*, 1977

Sometimes Jass thought it might be just as well that she never saw the places with names she liked. Royal Oak sounded like something out of Shakespeare, though probably it was nothing but a pub.

CATHERINE STORR, *The Underground Conspiracy*, 1987

Paddington
Change for Bakerloo, Circle and District lines

Amongst the last of the departing guests the fourth and fifth brothers [Forsyte], Nicholas and Roger, walked away together, directing their steps alongside Hyde Park towards the Praed Street [Paddington] Station of the Underground. . . .

They entered the station.

'What class are you going? I go second.'

'No second for me,' said Nicholas; 'you never know what you may catch.'

He took a first-class ticket to Notting Hill Gate; Roger a second to South Kensington. The train coming in a minute later, the two brothers parted and entered their respective compartments. Each felt aggrieved that the other had not modified his habits to secure his society a little longer; but as Roger voiced it in his thoughts:

'Always a stubborn beggar, Nick!'

And as Nicholas expressed it to himself:

'Cantankerous chap Roger always was!'

JOHN GALSWORTHY, *The Man of Property*, 1906

The Mole found himself placed next to Mr Badger, and, as the other two were still deep in river-gossip from which nothing could divert them, he took the opportunity to tell Badger how comfortable and home-like it all felt to him. 'Once well underground,' he said, 'you know exactly where you are. Nothing can happen to you, and nothing can get at you. You're entirely your own master, and you don't have to consult anybody or mind what they say. Things go on all the same overhead, and you let 'em, and don't bother about 'em. When you want to, up you go, and there the things are, waiting for you.'

The Badger simply beamed on him. 'That's exactly what I say,' he replied. 'There's no security, or peace and tranquillity, except underground. And then, if your ideas get larger and you wanted to expand – why, a dig and a scrape and there you are! If you feel your house is a bit too big, you stop up a hole or two, and there you are again! No builders, no tradesmen, no remarks passed on you by fellows looking over your wall, and, above all, no weather.'

KENNETH GRAHAME, *The Wind in the Willows*, 1908

Edgware Road
Change for District line

Mr. Sponge had gone along Oxford Street at a somewhat improved pace to his usual wont – had paused for a shorter period in the ''bus' perplexed 'Circus', and pulled up seldomer than usual between the Circus and the limits of his stroll. Behold him now at the Edgware Road end, eyeing the 'busses with a wanting-a-ride like air, instead of the contemptuous sneer he generally adopts towards those uncouth productions. Red, green, blue, drab, cinnamon-colour, passed and crossed, and jostled, and stopped, and blocked, and the cads telegraphed, and winked, and nodded, and smiled, and slanged, but Mr. Sponge regarded them not. He had a sort of ''bus' panorama in his head, knew the run of them all, whence they started, where they stopped, where they watered, where they changed, and wonderful to relate, had never been entrapped into a sixpenny fare when he meant to take a threepenny one. In cab and ''bus' geography there is not a more learned man in London.

R.S. SURTEES, *Mr Sponge's Sporting Tour*, 1853

Baker Street
Change for Bakerloo, Jubilee and Metropolitan lines

One night – it was on the 20th of March, 1888 – I was returning from a journey to a patient (for I had now returned to civil practice), when my way led me through Baker-street. As I passed the well-remembered door, which must always be associated in my mind with my wooing, and with the dark incidents of the Study in Scarlet, I was seized with a keen desire to see Holmes again, and to know how he was employing his extraordinary powers. His rooms were brilliantly lit, and, even as I looked up, I saw his tall spare figure pass twice in a dark silhouette against the blind. He was pacing the room swiftly, eagerly, with his head sunk upon his chest, and his hands clasped behind him. To me, who knew his every mood and habit, his attitude and manner told their own story. He was at work again. He had arisen out of his drug-created dreams, and was hot upon the scent of some new problem. I rang the bell, and was shown up to the chamber which had formerly been in part my own.

SIR ARTHUR CONAN DOYLE, 'A Scandal in Bohemia',
The Adventures of Sherlock Holmes, 1892

Great Portland Street

James Boswell died in a house on the site of No. 122 in 1795 and Carl Maria von Weber at No. 91 in 1826. Leigh Hunt lived at No. 98 in 1812, and David Wilkie at No. 117 in 1808–9.

The London Encyclopaedia edited by Ben Weinreb
and Christopher Hibbert, 1983

Euston Square

'We must be running late,' the passengers had been saying from time to time, uncertainly glancing at one another as though the feeling of lateness might be subjective, then at the blinded windows of the carriage. 'Whereabouts would we be now? – how far are we along?' Now and then somebody in a corner prised at a blind's edge, put an eye to the crack – but it was useless; Midland canals and hedges were long gone from view; not a hill or tower showed through the drape of night; every main-line landmark was blotted out. Only a loud catastrophic roar told them, even, when they were in a tunnel. But by now speed had begun to slacken; from the sound of the train, more and more often constricted deep in cuttings between and under walls, they must be entering London: no other city's built-up density could be so strongly felt. . . . Euston. All the way down the train doors burst open while the inky ribbon of platform still slipped by. Nobody could wait for the train to stop; everybody was hurling themselves on London.

ELIZABETH BOWEN, *The Heat of the Day*, 1949

King's Cross St. Pancras
Change for Northern, Piccadilly and Victoria lines

June 10, 1769. Advertisement [placed by John Armstrong].

St. Pancras Wells Waters are in the greatest perfection, and highly recommended by the most eminent physicians in the kingdom. To prevent mistakes, St. Pancras Wells is on that side the churchyard towards London; the house and gardens of which are as genteel and rural as any round this metropolis; the best of tea, coffee, and hot loaves, every day, may always be depended on, with neat wines, curious punch, Dorchester, Marlborough and Ringwood beers; Burton, Yorkshire, and other fine ales and cyder; and also cows kept to accommodate ladies and gentlemen with new milk and cream, and syllabubs in the greatest perfection.

W. THORNBURY AND E. WALFORD, *Old and New London*, 1873–8

Farringdon

Once on a stall in Farringdon Road I found
An atlas folio of great lithographs,
Views of Ionian Isles, flyleaf inscribed
By Edward Lear – and bought it for a bob.
Perhaps one day I'll find a 'first' of Keats,
Wedged between Goldsmith and *The Law of Torts;*
Perhaps – but that was not the reason why
Untidy bookshops gave me such delight.
It was the smell of books, the plates in them,
Tooled leather, marbled paper, gilded edge . . .

JOHN BETJEMAN, *Summoned by Bells,* 1960

Barbican

[John Milton] was buried in the same grave as his father at St Giles
Without Cripplegate, a much damaged and much restored medieval
church in the modern Barbican.

IAN OUSBY, *Literary Britain and Ireland,* 1990

Moorgate
Change for Northern line

June 23rd 1887. I had my first experience of Hades to-day, and if the
real thing is to be like that I shall never again do anything wrong. I got
into the Underground railway at Baker Street. I wanted to go to
Moorgate Street in the City. . . . The compartment in which I sat was
filled with passengers who were smoking pipes, as is the British habit,
and as the smoke and sulphur from the engine fill the tunnel, all the
windows have to be closed. The atmosphere was a mixture of sulphur,
coal dust and foul fumes from the oil lamp above; so that by the time
we reached Moorgate Street I was near dead of asphyxiation and heat.
I should think these Underground railways must soon be discontinued,
for they are a menace to health. A few minutes earlier can be no con-
sideration, since hansom cabs and omnibuses, carried by the swiftest
horses I have seen anywhere, do the work most satisfactorily.

R.D. BLUMENFELD, *R.D.B.'s Diary, 1887–1914,* 1930

Liverpool Street

Change for Central, Circle and Metropolitan lines

Ben did not go straight home from Liverpool Street Station. This was the last day of the boys' summer holidays, when Mrs Blewitt always gave them a treat. That was why she had brought Frankie and Paul to meet Ben. They all went straight to have baked beans on toast in the station Help-Yourself that overlooks the comings and goings of the trains.

PHILIPPA PEARCE, *A Dog So Small*, 1962

Aldgate East

Change for District line

The Saxons called it Ealdgate, old gate. It was rebuilt at some time between 1108 and 1147. In 1215, the year of Magna Carta, the Barons came through it on their way to lay siege to the Tower.

The London Encyclopaedia edited by Ben Weinreb
and Christopher Hibbert, 1983

Whitechapel

Change for District line

And away went the coach up Whitechapel, to the admiration of the whole population of that pretty densely-populated quarter.

'Not a wery nice neighbourhood this, Sir,' said Sam, with the touch of the hat which always preceded his entering into conversation with his master.

'It is not indeed, Sam,' replied Mr Pickwick, surveying the crowded and filthy street through which they were passing.

'It's a wery remarkable circumstance, Sir,' said Sam, 'that poverty and oysters always seems to go together.'

'I don't understand you, Sam,' said Mr Pickwick.

'What I mean, Sir,' said Sam, 'is, that the poorer a place is, the greater call there seems to be for oysters. Look here, Sir; here's a oyster stall to every half-dozen houses – the street's lined with 'em. Blessed if I don't think that ven a man's wery poor, he rushes out of his lodgings, and eats oysters in reg'lar desperation.'

'To be sure he does,' said Mr Weller senior, 'and it's just the same vith pickled salmon!'

'Those are two very remarkable facts, which never occurred to me before,' said Mr Pickwick. 'The very first place we stop at, I'll make a note of them.'

CHARLES DICKENS, *The Pickwick Papers*, 1836–7

All day I loafed in the streets, east as far as Wapping, west as far as Whitechapel. It was queer after Paris; everything was so much cleaner and quieter and drearier. . . . The crowds were better dressed and the faces comelier and milder and more alike, without that fierce individuality of the French. . . . It was the land of the tea urn and the Labour Exchange, as Paris is the land of the bistro and the sweatshop.

GEORGE ORWELL, *Down and Out in Paris and London*, 1933

In peak hours this line continues up to Barking.

ACKNOWLEDGEMENTS

We would like to thank our families and friends who have helped us over the years during the preparation of this book, especially Sandy Marriage, Robin Ollington, Bryan Rooney, Suzanne St Albans, Anthony Sampson, Kathleen Tillotson, Malcolm Holmes of the Camden Local History Library and the staff of the North Reading Room, British Library.

The compilers and publishers gratefully acknowledge permission to reproduce the following copyright material in this book:

J.S. Bain: *A Bookseller Looks Back,* © J.S. Bain 1940. Reprinted by permission of Macmillan London.

Julian Barnes: *Metroland,* © Julian Barnes 1980. Reprinted by permission of Jonathan Cape.

John Betjeman: 'City' (*Continual Dew* 1937) and 'The Metropolitan Railway – Baker Street Station Buffet' from *Collected Poems,* © John Betjeman 1958. *Summoned by Bells,* © John Betjeman 1960. Reprinted by permission of John Murray.

Mary Cathcart Borer: *The City of London: A History,* © Mary Cathcart Borer 1977. Reprinted by permission of Constable.

Elizabeth Bowen: *The Heat of the Day,* © Elizabeth Bowen 1949. Reprinted by permission of Jonathan Cape.

Peter Bushell: *London's Secret History,* © Peter Bushell 1983. Reprinted by permission of Constable.

Peter Carey: *Oscar and Lucinda,* © Peter Carey 1988. Reprinted by permission of Faber & Faber.

Hugh Casson: *Hugh Casson's London,* © Hugh Casson 1983. Reprinted by permission of John Johnson.

Gavin Ewart: 'Tennysonian Reflections at Barnes Bridge' from *Londoners,* © Gavin Ewart 1964. Reprinted by permission of William Heinemann.

Leigh Hatts: *Country Walks around London,* © Leigh Hatts 1983. Reprinted by permission of David & Charles.

ACKNOWLEDGEMENTS

Philip Howard: 'Wapping' and 'Philip Howard looks at London' from *The Times*, © Times Newspapers. Reprinted by permission of Times Newspapers.

Alan A. Jackson: *London's Metropolitan Railway*, © Alan A. Jackson 1986. Reprinted by permission of David & Charles.

John Mortimer: *Clinging to the Wreckage*, © John Mortimer 1982. Reprinted by permission of Weidenfeld & Nicolson.

George Orwell: *Down and Out in Paris and London*, © George Orwell 1933. Reprinted by permission of A.M. Heath on behalf of the estate of Sonia Brownell Orwell, published by Martin Secker & Warburg.

Ian Ousby: *Literary Britain and Ireland*, © Ian Ousby 1990. Reprinted by permission of A. & C. Black.

Philippa Pearce: *A Dog So Small*, © Philippa Pearce 1962. Reprinted by permission of Constable.

Nikolaus Pevsner: *The Buildings of England: Hertfordshire* (second edition revised by Bridget Cherry 1977), © Nikolaus Pevsner 1953, and Nikolaus Pevsner and Bridget Cherry 1977. Reprinted by permission of Penguin Books.

J.B. Priestley: *Adam in the Moonshine*, © J.B. Priestley 1927. Reprinted by permission of Peters, Fraser & Dunlop.

C.H. Rolph: *London Particulars*, © C.H. Rolph 1980. Published by Oxford University Press. Reprinted by permission of David Higham Associates.

Muriel Spark: *Curriculum Vitae*, © Muriel Spark 1992. Reprinted by permission of David Higham Associates.

Catherine Storr: *The Underground Conspiracy*, © Catherine Storr 1987. Reprinted by permission of Peters, Fraser & Dunlop.

Barbara Vine: *King Solomon's Carpet*, © Kingsmarkham Enterprises Ltd 1991. Reprinted by permission of Penguin Books.

Ben Weinreb and Christopher Hibbert: *The London Encyclopaedia*, © Ben Weinreb and Christopher Hibbert 1983. Reprinted by permission of Macmillan London.

H.G. Wells: *Love and Mr Lewisham*, © H.G. Wells 1900. Reprinted by permission of A.P. Watt on behalf of The Literary Executors of the Estate of H.G. Wells.

W. Wheatley: *History of Edward Latymer and His Foundations*, © W. Wheatley 1936. Reprinted by permission of Cambridge University Press.

The publishers have made every effort to contact copyright holders where they can be found. The publishers will be happy to include any missing copyright acknowledgements in future editions.